MW00795967

TRADING VOLATILITY

USING CORRELATION, TERM STRUCTURE AND SKEW:

Learn to successfully trade VIX, UVXY, TVIX, VXXB & SVXY

Seth Goldman

Published by Stanford Publishing
stanfordpub.com

CONTENTS

CHAPTER 1: Volatility

Why invest in volatility?

It is crucial to have a good understanding of what volatility is and how volatility instruments behave to successfully navigate and invest in the growing volatility landscape. Alternative assets like volatility can offer investors an important source of investment diversification, help boost a portfolio's return, and offer a low correlation to traditional assets.

What is volatility?

First, let's understand what people mean when they refer to volatility.

Realized Volatility

Realized volatility is a measurement of historical volatility. This is the volatility that actually happened in the past but the calculation is time frame dependent which can be confusing. For example, realized volatility could refer to the daily returns of the last ten days, monthly returns for the last year, or even yearly returns for the last ten years. Frequently traders quote an annualized thirty day realized volatility.

Implied Volatility

Implied volatility is the option market's expectation for volatility over a period in the future - usually stated in annualized terms. Whereas realized volatility is determined from historical price returns, implied volatility is forward looking and is calculated from option prices. This is the measure of volatility that underlies the VIX Index, as well as the measure that people look to trade.

What is the VIX?

The VIX Index is the most popular measure of implied volatility. Specifically, the volatility implied by a portfolio of 30 day S&P 500 Index options.

Often referred to as the 'fear index' or simply 'the VIX', the index represents the market's expectation of equity volatility. While the VIX Index itself is not tradable, index futures give hedgers and investors an imperfect proxy exposure to the Index. VIX futures represent the market's best collective guess at the value of the VIX Index at their expiry.

Where do returns come from?

Volatility investment returns come from two separate but related sources:

Volatility Risk Premium (VRP)

Volatility Risk Premium is the premium hedgers pay over realized volatility for S&P 500 Index options.

The premium stems from hedgers paying to insure their portfolios, and manifests itself in the difference between the price at which options are sold (implied volatility) and the volatility that the S&P 500 ultimately realizes (realized volatility).

Futures Risk Premium (FRP)

VIX Futures Risk Premium is the further premium hedgers pay for VIX futures over the VIX Index itself. This premium is often referred to as 'contango', and can be seen in the tendency for longer dated VIX futures to trade at a premium to the VIX Index.

Volatility investing is like selling insurance

Volatility investing should not be confused with volatility hedging. Just like you pay insurance premiums to protect your home against damage; market participants pay volatility premiums to protect against a market crash. Like insurance companies, volatility investors can systematically harvest this premium.

It is important to remember that insurance companies also make payouts after adverse events, and volatility investors may experience similar drawdowns during spikes in volatility. It is for this reason that volatility investing should only be viewed from a long term perspective and as diversification to traditional portfolios. Like insurance companies, volatility investors shoulder risk in the short term to harvest risk premium over the long term.

Manage risk

As the name implies, volatility returns can be volatile during times of market turmoil, and properly managing risk is key to a successful investment. Along with intensive analytical and technical analysis, here are a few key points to keep in mind:

Maintain a Long Term Perspective

Volatility investing is not a get rich quick scheme. It is an asset class that offers an intriguing risk-return profile. Like any asset class, it should be thoughtfully placed in your asset allocation and outsourced to professionals if you are not constantly monitoring it.

Properly Diversify

On top of a diversified asset allocation, diversifying your volatility investment across term structures, volatility products, volatility strategies, and geographies can help smooth returns and improve your risk adjusted retunes.

Be Proactive

To keep Volatility Risk Premium and Futures Risk Premium in your favor, it is imperative to remain systematic, properly scale your exposure, and be willing to move into cash frequently and often.

CHAPTER 2: VIX and VIX Futures

Volatility has recently become a very popular asset class among major investment banks and sophisticated investment funds because it is able to generate large returns as well as hedge risk.

The unique mean-reverting property of volatility makes it possible to generate forecasts that can be used to take advantage of spikes and declines in volatility. By tracking and analyzing a variety of volatility-related indices and metrics, the direction of future moves in volatility funds can be made with reasonable accuracy.

These forecasts provide us with an edge in the stock market and we use them as the foundation of our trading strategy.

In order to understand our approach to trading volatility exchange traded products (ETPs) it is important to understand what the VIX tracks and the concept of VIX futures.

Most simply stated, the VIX measures the expected volatility of the S&P 500 Index (SPX). By taking a weighted average of a range of put and call options[1] for the SPX, the

------

1

Implied Volatility

VIX obtains a value that provides the market's expectations for the dispersion of the S&P 500 (up or down) for the next 30 days. Because the VIX is a weighted average calculation of options, it is not directly tradable. Note that the VIX is also sometimes referred to as "spot VIX" or "30 day implied volatility."

The value of the VIX is often quoted as a price but actually represents a percentage on an annualized basis. For example, a VIX of 16 means that market participants expect the SPX to move at an annualized rate of 16% over the next 30 days.

Sometimes it is easier to think about the VIX on a shorter timeframe to help put it in context of daily market moves. To express VIX in a monthly rate you can divide its value by $\sqrt{12}$, which equals 4.6% for a VIX of 16.

Note that when talking about the VIX, the phrase "market participants expect" means that movement occurs with a 68% probability (one standard deviation). While it is not necessary for the purpose of trading to go into more details of the calculation, you can check out CBOE's white paper on VIX if you are interested in the math behind it all.

VIX Futures

In addition to the VIX there are also VIX futures. While spot VIX is a calculation of the current 30-day implied volatility of SPX, VIX futures are the expected value of the VIX on the expiration date for a given month. VIX futures are contracts that can be bought or sold directly.

Each month has its own VIX futures contracts and when we

look at the group of VIX futures together we get something
called the term structure.

Normally the term structure is shaped such that VIX futures
that have a longer time to expiration are more expensive
than nearer months, a condition known as contango. The
reason for this pricing structure is that a longer timeframe
translates into greater uncertainty of what price VIX might
be   on   those   expiration   dates.
A term structure that has near term months that are more
expensive than more distant months is in backwardation.
This condition happens when market participants believe
that
the current levels of volatility are excessively high based on
historical norms and they anticipate that VIX will revert to a
value   closer   to   long   term   averages.

The exact shape of the term structure changes daily. In
order to monitor how the term structure changes over time
I like to look at a chart showing the daily closing values of
VIX and each month of VIX futures over a multi-month
timeframe.

vixcentral.com offer a good multi-month chart

CHAPTER 3:

FUNDAMENTAL CONCEPTS AND STRATEGIES FORTRADING VOLATILITY ETPS

By viewing the VIX futures term structure we can see a few things more clearly:

• Contango, the condition in which contracts for near term months are less expensive than contracts further out in the future, is clearly visible at most points.

• VIX futures months advance forward one month (second month becomes the first month, third becomes the second month, etc.) and a new seventh month is added into the mix.

• As time progresses the values of more distant VIX futures months approach spot VIX. VIX futures and the difference between it and spot VIX gradually decreases as it approaches its expiration date.

While the term structure is in contango most of the time there are also times of backwardation, which is visible in the chart of VIX futures between August 2008 and February 2009. Here we see VIX is greater than Oct, which is greater than Nov, which is greater than Dec, etc.

The edge in trading VIX futures ETPs comes from the fact that each fund has a daily rolling mechanism to maintain a targeted maturity.

In order to accomplish that target the fund will own a blend of two or more months of VIX futures. Each day, the fund sells a portion of its existing holdings of VIX futures and buys a replacement amount of the next month VIX futures. A significant difference between the prices of the two months of futures creates a measurable directional pull, which can be thought of as a headwind or tailwind for the security. Technically known as the roll yield, this headwind can be positive, negative, or neutral. Our goal in trading VIX ETPs is to make the trades which give us the highest probability to make a profitable trade, and a key piece of information is the direction and magnitude of the roll yield.

There are a variety of VIX futures ETPs, each targeting a specific objective. I choose to focus on both long volatility and short volatility funds that have a price replication target of either short-term VIX futures (months one and two) or mid-term VIX futures (months four to seven).

Long Volatility

One of the most popular VIX-related funds is iPath's "VIX Short-term Futures ETN" (ticker symbol: VXXB) which tracks the daily movement of the first and second month VIX   futures
and provides a return of the daily gain or loss of those VIX futures.

Short Volatility

The funds that allow investors to take the opposite side of the   trade   and   "short"   volatility   to
obtain a return which is the daily inverse of VXX are the "VelocityShares   Daily   Inverse   VIX
Short-Term ETN" XIV[2] and the "Proshares Short VIX Short-term   futures   ETP"   (ticker   symbol: SVXY).

Mid-Term Funds

For some people the daily movements in VXXB and SVXY create too much volatility in their portfolio.

One of my favorite alternatives to SVXY is the "VelocityShares Daily Inverse VIX Short-Term ETN" (ticker symbol: ZIV), which allows you to short volatility of months that are
4-7 months in the future. Generally, VIX futures that have a longer time to expiration will move less on a given day than VIX futures that are closer to expiration, making ZIV a less volatile product.

---

2   XIV Close on Feb 2018 after a +90% one day loss

Impact Of The Roll Yield

How important is it to know the direction and magnitude of a fund's roll yield? Consider VXX[3]. It launched on Jan 30, 2009 at $6,693 (adjusted for reverse splits) and has fallen to $42.55 as of the end of 2013. During this same timeframe VIX has fallen from 44.84. to 13.73, a 69% loss. However, VXX has lost 99.3% of its value -- a result of a persistent contango and negative roll yield.

A negative roll yield for VXX means a positive roll yield for its inverse funds.

The strong VXX[4] losses and XIV gains are primarily a result of a persistent contango term structure during much of this

---

3   On Feb 2019, VXX change to VXXB
4   On Feb 2019, VXX change to VXXB

timeframe. However, a contango term structure and these types of gains should never be taken as a given. What makes this product dangerous to the uninformed investor is that the roll yield can reverse to negative and cause large drawdowns.

Notice in August 2011 as XIV fell from $19 to $5, losing nearly 75% of its value. This loss was a direct result of the roll yield changing from negative to positive as the term structure switched to backwardation. Conversely, the roll yield for VXX changed from negative to positive and it became quite profitable to buy VXX during this time.

ZIV is also impacted by a roll yield but by a lesser amount. The overall performance of ZIV follows a similar trend as XIV but the magnitude of its moves is smaller.

Clearly these securities provide great opportunities for investors if you know what to look for. They can also be dangerous if used incorrectly or if an investor does not pay attention to the VIX futures term structure. This is why this book and our investments management service is dedicated to tracking and analyzing the term structure data.

Value Of The Roll Yield

To understand the roll yield we have to dig into the details of the monthly roll cycle.

Summarizing the roll process for VXXB:

1. At the beginning of the roll period all the weight is allocated to the first month futures contract.

2. On each subsequent business day a fraction of the first month VIX futures holding is sold and an equal notional amount of the second month VIX futures is bought. The exact quantity bought/sold depends on the number of business days in the roll
period (the number of days varies but averages out to about 21).

3. The next roll period starts after all weight from the front month has been sold and the old second month VIX futures contract becomes the new first month VIX futures contract. The process then repeats.

This process generates a roll yield headwind or tailwind depending on the difference in price between the two months of VIX futures.

Roll Yield During Contango

When the term structure is in contango the fund is selling units of first month VIX futures and using the proceeds to purchase a quantity of second month VIX futures at a higher value. The "buy high, sell low" scenario results is a negative roll yield for VXXB.

Roll Yield During Backwardation

When the term structure is in backwardation the fund is selling units of first month VIX futures and using the proceeds to purchase a quantity of second month VIX futures at a lower value. The "buy low, sell high" scenario results is a positive roll yield for VXXB.

Magnitude

The actual size of the monthly roll yield depends on the difference between and first and second month VIX futures -- a larger difference means a stronger roll yield. An approximate
value is obtained simply by using the price of the relevant VIX futures in the standard percentage gain/loss calculation.

Therefore we need to divide the monthly roll yield by the number of weeks in the roll period, which is typically between 4 and 5. Given any monthly roll yield, a roll period with 5 weeks would have a smaller weekly roll yield than a roll period with 4 weeks.

Inverse And Mid-Term Products

The same process applies to inverse VIX futures products except the buying and selling is reversed. In order to obtain a value of the roll yield for the inverse products (XIV and SVXY) just change the negative sign in the VXXB roll yield to a positive, or vice versa.

The mid-term VIX futures ETPs use a similar process except they are buying and selling a fraction of fourth and seventh month VIX futures while holding 33% of fifth month and 33% of sixth month futures.

Historical Values

Historically the roll yields as calculated above have fallen into the ranges outlined below.
The maximum and minimum values are fairly extreme but it is still possible that roll yields could exceed these values in the future. Below are the average, standard deviation, lowest, and highest values of the weekly roll yields for XIV (past 11 years) and ZIV

Plotting the daily closing values of the weekly roll yield for VXXB provides further insight into typical roll yield values and how it changes on a daily basis.

22

Optimizing Trading Performance Using Bias Indicators

In general, buying VIX futures ETPs when their roll yield is positive will allow an investor to do pretty well in trading these products along with their trends. The roll yield is a critical
piece of information for trading volatility ETPs but does not tell the entire story. The headwind or tailwind from the roll yield can often be overwhelmed by a strong opposing move in the underlying VIX futures. In fact, trading only based on the direction of the roll yield will result in vast underperformance against a buy-and-hold approach when there   are
only brief periods of backwardation as we've seen during the   past   years.

Because of this problem, the roll yield is only one component of our forecasts. We take additional daily inputs to measure key momentum and state changes to generate our
proprietary Bias indicators, providing a more holistic view of the directional force of a volatility fund. This provides us with a signal-based system to place better swing trades instead of blindly following the term structure or leaving our portfolio excessively vulnerable with a buy-and-hold approach.

CHAPTER 4: The Exchange Traded Product That Lost 99% Of Its Value

The most popular way to play volatility is going to its grave on on Jan. 30, 2019, but the impending death of an exchange-traded note sold by Barclays Plc is not the end of the story for futures traders.

The iPath S&P 500 VIX Short-Term Futures ETN, ticker VXX, mature as scheduled on Jan. 30, ending a favored means to bet on a gauge of expected gyrations in the S&P 500 Index. Anyone still owning the note at maturity will receive a cash payment based on its indicative value at the previous session's close.

It's a mixed legacy -- due to a structural quirk, the note lost 99 percent of its value over its life -- but it also democratized investor access to implied U.S. equity volatility. And there exists the potential, however slight at this point, for the wind-down to create one last wave in the futures market, if Barclays is forced to liquidate its hedge for the almost $500 million still invested in the note by January 29, 2019.

The bank is replacing VXX with VXXB, a note identical in almost everything but ticker and maturity date, but shifting assets and trading volume to the replacement has proved slow, and memories of exchange-traded products fueling market turmoil are still fresh, prompting caution.

VXX holders move to its replacement, VXXB

While VXX still had more shares outstanding than VXXB, the pace of the transition has accelerated. The most recent data shows assets have dropped to $488 million, as VXXB's have climbed, down from $920 million one week ago and an average of $950 million throughout the fourth quarter. Likewise, the dollar volume traded in the two products has converged.

Volume convergence for VXX and VXXB

The eleventh-hour transition isn't necessarily indicative of a large swath of holders having fallen asleep at the switch. The last expiration date for futures on VXX was Friday, and dealers or market makers who held the note to hedge themselves against an option they'd written would likely have looked to maintain that exposure through Friday.

But if some traders fear a lumpy exit today, they could look to sell VIX futures or options before the close to front-run the expected impact of a large sale, or enact spread strategies to bet on a pick-up in the implied volatility of implied volatility.

The dollar value of futures contracts that XIV, the now-defunct VelocityShares Daily Inverse VIX Short-Term ETN, was required to buy rose by billions in just a matter of 15 minutes during the chaotic session that felled the product. By comparison, a couple hundred million dollars worth of VIX futures hangs in the balance with VXX's well-telegraphed exit.

"The odds of a disruption are very low, but you never know, and there might be some people who are going to speculate on that,".

Volumes down on VXX after final option expiration date

Barclays is the largest owner of VXX, according to data compiled by Bloomberg. The firm lends out its shares to investors who want to bet against VXX, earning a fee in return.

VXX's prospectus warns that the product is only suitable for "a very short investment horizon" -- and with good reason: The note will mature having lost more than 99 percent of its value.

That's because the note's rebalancing strategy involved consistently selling front-month contracts to purchase second-month contracts to be prepared for the contract's roll. Generally, the VIX futures curve is upward-sloping –- in so-called contango –- because the outlook for U.S. stocks is generally more uncertain over longer periods of time, so the roll eats into returns.

For that reason, it was heavily shorted by traders -- a functionality that was slow to come to some brokerages for VXXB -- which also may have contributed to the glacial migration.

Ironically, XIV -- which blew up spectacularly -- ultimately vastly outperformed VXX over its lifetime, proving for some that Neil Young's maxim still holds: It's better to burn out than to fade away.

Vol-linked notes will always die

CHAPTER 5:

The Difference between Volatility Risk Premium and VIX Futures Premium

Beyond the simpler questions, like whether or not the VIX is an investable index (it is of course not), there seemed to be a general misunderstanding of where the returns in popular VIX linked Exchange Traded Products (ETPs) like SVXY and ZIV come from. This misunderstanding seems to stem from a confusion of terms like contango, roll yield, Volatility Risk Premium (VRP), and Futures Risk Premium (FRP). This chapter will explain the source of these returns by more clearly describing the difference between VRP and FRP.

These products 'roll futures', and that this roll does not affect their returns, but instead their returns frequently arise from the inevitable changes in value of the VIX futures themselves – a change in value that could be better described as 'contango decay' than 'roll yield'.

'Contango decay' can be thought of as the steady decline of VIX futures prices towards the value of the VIX Index - or as some would argue – the pull of the VIX Index towards the VIX futures. I won't go into the arguments for and against either interpretation, but suffice it to say the first argument relies on the relationship between traditional investable commodities and their futures and ignores the 'uninvestability' of the VIX Index, while the latter relies on the Vega weights of the portfolio of options that the VIX Index references compared with the portfolio that the futures reference. It's important to remember that the VIX Index has the only futures underlying that is totally

27

uninvestable and this facet alone gives the behavior of its futures some surprising characteristics.

So what is this contango decay and is it the same as VRP? Well simply put, no! Contango decay is a characteristic of futures prices while VRP is a characteristic of options markets – including options on the S&P 500. It's perhaps helpful to think how there's contango decay in oil futures that no one would ever describe as VRP. The confusion of these two terms can cause investors to make poor decisions when investing in VIX, and properly understanding the difference can help investors better utilize these products.

In contrast to FRP, VRP is the premium paid by option buyers to insure their portfolios. Often quoted in terms of volatility points, it is the difference between implied volatility (the price of options in volatility terms) and realized volatility (the volatility an investor actually experiences). This premium is frequently positive, i.e investors frequently pay several vol points more for options than the volatility they realize. For option buyers this is the cost of insurance, for option sellers this is VRP.

So VRP is an options market phenomenon, the outcome of option buyers willing to pay away a premium to hold a hedge or insurance over their portfolios. Priced in vol points, this premium does find its way into the VIX futures market but not as FRP as some assume.

By way of explanation it is useful to take a step back. The VIX Index is one measure of implied volatility, and represents the average implied volatility of a portfolio of options expiring in 30 days' time. As a measure of implied volatility, the VIX Index is a useful way of gauging the price (in volatility terms) that investors are willing to pay to own portfolio insurance over the next 30 days. It is also a useful tool to estimate VRP.

A good estimate of historic VRP can be made by subtracting historical realized volatility from that implied by the VIX index. For example, if the previous 30 days have demonstrated an annualised volatility of just 10 volatility points, and the VIX Index was valued at 20 just 30 days ago, one could describe the 30 day historic VRP as 10 annualized vol points (20 implied – 10 realised). If the VIX remains unchanged and over the following 30 days the SPX actually realizes 15 vol points, one could describe the realized VRP as 5 (20 implied – 15 realized).

This VRP is traded actively in the S&P 500 options market through the daily gamma-theta relationship of options and the daily moves in the index. If daily moves exceed expectations, gamma gains on delta hedged option portfolios will exceed theta loses and visa versa. If traders expect realized volatility to rise they may be willing to pay more for options and visa versa.

So how does this relate to the VIX futures market? Well, VIX futures represent the market's expectation of the level of the VIX at that futures' expiry i.e it is the market's expectation of 30 day implied volatility sometime in the future. If expectations rise over time, so will the price of the futures and visa versa. This change in VIX futures prices is therefore the direct result of a change in expectations and frequently not the result of historic or realized volatility.

So if a VIX futures' value falls from say 15 to 10 over a month this is because the expected value of the VIX (the implied volatility of the S&P 500) has fallen and does not necessarily mean realized volatility has changed one way or another. This might occur for example if an upcoming market event results is an underwhelming response, that is to say as the event passes so does the expectation of future volatility, and this can occur with or without a realized volatility event.

So why are longer dated expectations of volatility so frequently higher than shorter dated expectations, i.e why are VIX futures so frequently priced higher than the VIX index itself? Well this relates to the shape of the S&P 500 options term structure, or the term structure of implied S&P 500 volatility.

The underlying market for most US equity volatility products is the S&P 500 Index, and it is demand for options and structured products linked to the S&P 500 that ultimately dictates the shape of that implied volatility curve. There are numerous products driving this shape as well as complex technical effects like interest rates on forward volatility, but two of the simplest influences are leverage and portfolio insurance, and demand for both of these play important roles in defining the shape of implied volatility curves.

Portfolio insurance is perhaps the most spoken about source of demand for options. Put simply, demand for portfolio insurance results from managers buying puts on stocks or their indexes to help protect their portfolios from downward moves. Their continued buying of puts and rolling these puts further and further out in time maintains a steady upward pressure on longer dated implied volatility.

The second, equally important influence but often

overlooked, is the demand for leverage. Buying unhedged options can give fund managers tremendous exposure to the market, while at the same time only risking the cost of their premium. This useful characteristic of options, coupled with the immense scale of the long only equity market creates a further demand for longer dated options and an upward pressure on implied volatility. The same applies for structured equity products issued by banks and insurance companies. Given the leverage available in options, structured products typically utilize options to take their long term equity exposure, thereby leaving more free cash to utilize on other exposures or to simply fund other areas of the bank.

So these are some of the reasons for an upward sloping S&P 500 implied volatility curve. But how does this upward sloping S&P 500 curve transpose to an upward sloping VIX futures curve? Well, it's useful to remember that the VIX Index and its futures are ultimately a reflection of S&P 500 implied volatility, and, as such, longer dated VIX futures are a reflection of longer dated S&P 500 implied volatility. A steep S&P 500 vol curve therefore frequently results in a steep VIX futures curve. Those of you who have read my earlier articles will know that this relationship is far from perfect as there is no true 'arbitrage' opportunity between VIX futures and SPX options, but despite this there are numerous proxy hedges that make this relationship strong.

So that explains why the VIX futures curve is frequently upward sloping and why a VIX FRP exists - longer dated VIX futures are priced higher because of a consistent demand for longer dated S&P 500 volatility products. But how is FRP realized in VIX linked ETPs. Well, simply through the passing of time. If 90 day VIX futures are priced at 20 vol points, and 60 day at just 15 then - all else being equal - those 90 day futures could be expected to decay to become 60 day futures in just 30 days – a decay of

31

5 vol points in 30 days or about 17bp of vol per day. Inverse VIX ETPs that track the inverse value of these futures would therefore benefit from these decaying futures, and as you'll now see can have little to do with the difference between implied and realized volatility of the S&P 500.

So why is it important to understand the difference between VRP and FRP? Well, FRP can exist whether VRP exists or not, or put another way, FRP and the corresponding decay in VIX linked ETPs, can exist whether or not implied S&P 500 volatility exceeds realized or not, and keeping an eye on FRP may be more important than VRP when choosing to buy or sell a VIX linked ETP.

CHAPTER 6: LESSONS FROM A HISTORY OF FINANCIAL DISASTERS

Most famous fund failures have *leverage* at their core. That's the true culprit for disaster — not the actual trade ideas. Bad position sizing kills.

Long Term Capital Management (LTCM) strategy involved scanning the world for bond spreads that diverged from historical values — something known as convergence trading. When spreads diverged from their means, LTCM would buy the cheap and sell the expensive bond. Then wait for prices to revert back to their "theoretical efficient" market price and make a small profit.

But LTCM wasn't satisfied with the tiny profits on the spread. They were "Masters of the Universe" and wanted to put up bigly numbers that smoked the S&P. So they took this simple strategy and leveraged up to high heaven.

Before LTCM was incinerated they had a portfolio market value of $129 billion. Of which, $125 billion was borrowed money. That's a leverage ratio of 32:1.

Once volatility hit the market, those bond spreads that LTCM had leveraged to infinity betting that they would quickly converge just like all previous times... kept diverging... and diverging. Until eventually LTCM was forced into liquidation.

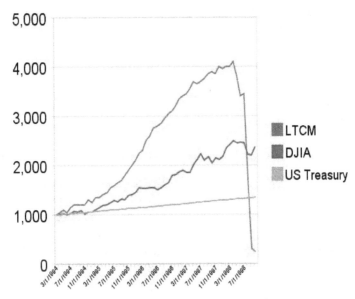

Leverage and crowding caused the forced unwind of the trade. Not the strategy of buying cheap bonds and selling expensive bonds.

LTCM had a good strategy that they ruined with excessive leverage.

The exact same leverage issue happened to Victor Niederhoffer in 1997.

After suffering from a huge loss on Thai stocks during the Thai Baht crisis, Niederhoffer turned to aggressive S&P 500 put writing in order to "make back" his losses.

Over the summer of 1997 he shorted out-of-the-money November 830 puts for prices between $4 and $6.
By October these puts were trading for just $0.60 and Niederhoffer had a large gain. But the Asian Contagion spread and eventually hit the S&P.

On Thursday October 23rd, 1997 the puts rose to $1.20. On Friday the S&P dropped further but closed well above Niederhoffer's option strike. Niederhoffer still wasn't worried — his puts were trading for $2.40.

Over the weekend Asian markets continued to sell off. Hong Kong dropped 5% during its session which triggered a risk off move in the US markets driving stocks down 7%. This rout continued into the next morning sending the S&P spiraling into the 800s.

Volatility skyrocketed. And Niederhoffer's puts shot up to $16. That's 300% higher than the price he sold them for.

Refco, Niederhoffer's broker at the time, was not happy. They called in his puts mid-morning on Tuesday October 28th for a loss of <u>$90 million</u>. Niederhoffer's $70 million fund turned into a capital blackhole of -$20 million.

The market bottomed right after Niederhoffer was margin called. By November, the market was back near highs. His 830 puts went on to expire worthless — meaning his trade, had he been able to hold on, turned out to be profitable.

But his leverage forced his liquidation. He was oversized and couldn't ride the trade out.

Niederhoffer had shorted so many puts that a run of the mill two-day market selloff sent him out on a stretcher.

If he had sized the trade correctly, he would have survived the ride and took home a small profit. But the guy was playing on tilt, got greedy, maybe a bit arrogant, and lost all of his client's money.

In his office he had, on a prominent wall, a painting of the Titanic, and in a interview he said that someday the market would do something utterly unexpected because in the world we live in something utterly unexpected always happens...

With the trading history books filled with examples like these where stupid sizing led to catastrophe you'd think trader's today would maybe, learn from the past. But of course that's not the case. Human nature is after all, human nature. And "easy" money is quite effective at clouding our better judgement.

In our case of Trading Volatility, The Volpocalype of 2018 showed us that both amateur and professional traders are still making the same mistakes with position size and leverage.

LJM partners, a mutual fund that sells options just like
Niederhoffer did and whose tagline was "superior returns
for the patient investor" followed the LTCM playbook.

A not-out-of-the-ordinary 10% fall in the S&P forced the
fund to close positions at extremely unfavorable prices.

And then there was this amatuer XIV trader from Reddit who lost nearly $4 million dollars in XIV, on Feb. 2018

Instrument	Qty	Mark	Mrk Chng	% Change	Net Liq	P/L Open	P/L Day	BP Effect
▸ SUNEQ	+235	.0101	0	0.00%	$2.37	($97.36)	$0.00	$0.00
▸ TVIX	-3,200	15.99	+8.49	+68.00%	($51,168.00)	$151,081.60	($27,168.00)	($102,336.00)
▸ XIV	+11,000	34.30	-81.25	-14.32%	$377,300.00	($1,074,200.00)	($1,100,552.35)	$0.00
▸ XIV	+10,056	34.30	-81.25	-14.32%	$344,920.80	($980,555.20)	($1,038,107.50)	$0.00
					$671,055.17	($1,903,770.96)	($2,165,827.85)	($102,336.00)
						($1,903,770.96)	($2,165,827.85)	($102,336.00)
							Cash & Sweep Vehicle: ($226,246.64)	
							OVERALL P/L YTD: ($3,706,009.43)	

XIV goes up over time. But it also has incredibly nasty drawdowns that can exceed 90%. It has the ability to go up 100s of percent but also the ability to go down 90-100%.

and another case study was "James Cordier" of optionsellers.com who blow up on Nov. 2018

Option Sellers, LLC was a Tampa, Florida based Registered Investment Adviser and CTA (Commodity Trading Adviser). They managed money for 290 clients. Considering the minimum investment was $250,000 and most investors likely had more money with them, I'd surmise that they were managing around $150m. On November 15, 2018, they informed their investors that not only was all their money lost but that clients would likely owe more money.

Quite intriguingly, their strategy imploded over the span of just a few trading days. And just to be sure, this wasn't fraud a la Bernie Madoff but investors actually lost their money "fair and square" if there is such a thing. Is this something all option sellers should worry about? Yes, if you are as reckless as Option Sellers. If you had bothered to check what these clowns were doing it was clear that this debacle was all but unavoidable. Let's take a look at what they did and the obvious mistakes that lead to the meltdown...

Well, it's in their name; they were selling options. Option Sellers quite correctly pointed out that most options expire worthless and option buyers tend to overpay for the insurance value of the options they purchase (on average, at least). Option Sellers made an investment strategy out of this well-documented observation and implemented it through what's called a short-strangle: selling both a Put and Call option with the strike prices spaced out so that the put strike is (significantly) below the call strike price. If the price of the underlying stays between the two strike prices you make the maximum profit at expiration!

Profit and loss profile of a short strangle. The speculator hopes that the price of the underlying security stays between the two strike prices for maximum profit.

OptionSellers did this strategy for a wide range of options on commodity futures contracts (oil, gas, gold, soybeans, etc.). How did they blow up then? Very simple, the short strangle involves a short call option and the potential loss of that position is unlimited. In November, Natural Gas future spiked and created a loss large enough to wipe out the entire equity. It's that simple. It has a similar flavor as the Credit Suisse Short-VIX ETN (Ticker XIV, now defunct) that I warned about in 2017 and that indeed shut down in February after it lost more than 90%. Most of that in one day!

End of story? Well, even a risky strategy like that can be managed properly by experienced finance professionals if they act responsibly. But the folks at OptionSellers did not. Here are the five steps that blew up the Option Sellers strategy:

1: Ignore the Option Greeks, especially Delta, Gamma and Vega!

I'm not really too surprised when retail options traders are completely oblivious to option math. But it's astonishing when professional money managers ignore simple option math, too. For example, Option Sellers marketed their approach with the compelling spiel "Hey, the underlying simply has to stay within the two strike prices and we make the maximum profit!"

Anyone with even a little bit of options trading experience has to cringe hearing that. It's demonstrably false and here's the perfect example: I got the portfolio snapshot from one poor twitter user @waklyn1 who posted his actual positions, see this link to his Google Sheet. We noticed that the Natural Gas futures price never even went beyond most of the strike prices. The futures price went to about 4.75 on November 14, while the short call strikes were mostly above $5, some even as high as $6.50. How did they still get wiped out?. It's for one particular short call option with a February 2019 expiration and a strike of $5.25. On November 8, this contract was trading at $0.05, and if this contract had been held to expiration the maximum profit would have been 10,000 times that amount, equal to $500.00 (that's because the underlying futures contract has a multiplier of 10,000). The underlying never even breached the strike price of $5.25, but the short position still racked up massive losses of about $7,000, which is about 14 times the maximum one could have earned if held to expiration.

Even though the underlying didn't breach the strike price, the short Call racked up massive losses!

So, this is the dirty little secret that OptionSellers didn't mention in their sales pitch: The underlying doesn't have to move beyond the strike prices and you still lose your money. (margin call or force liquidation)

That's because prior to the expiration, the option price doesn't give a damn about the blue P&L line at expiration. Instead, your P&L moves in response to changes in the underlying through the three major, relatively predictable channels, related to the option Greeks: for every point the underlying moves up, your short Call loses a certain amount (option Delta),this option delta increases, so the losses become successively more painful the higher the underlying moves (option Gamma), and in stress periods the option implied volatility moves up (option Vega), which further exacerbates the losses of the short call.

Not knowing how quickly the short call can rack up losses and only praying that the underlying doesn't move past the strikes is a recipe for disaster!

Solution: Know your option math! It's not that difficult. I recommend our book "A Better Option: Strategies for Stocks, Options, and Futures Trading by Interactive Financial" a standard reference for anything derivatives-related.

2: Use way too much leverage (size kill)

Warren Buffett warns that three things will have the potential to wipe out your wealth: Ladies, Liquor and Leverage. Just as a side note, that's funny because Buffett himself uses leverage to juice up returns as pointed out by the smart folks at AQR:

"One of the ways that Berkshire Hathaway was able to add so much return above that of the market is Berkshire's access to cheap leverage via its insurance business, allowing it to harvest greater amounts of these style exposures than most traditional investors could."

So, clearly, Buffett isn't against leverage per se, just against too much leverage. And I couldn't agree more! How much leverage were they using at OptionSellers? Again, back to the poor twitter user I mentioned above. He had around $400k with them but in his Google Sheet, he scaled up the positions to mimic the positions of a $1,000,000 portfolio. Not sure exactly why he did that, but so be it. The Option Sellers strategy piled up a spectacular loss of a just a little bit over $1,000,000 in the trading days between November 8 and November 14. It looks like the short Nat Gas call options were all forced into liquidation by the exchange on November 14 when the large jump in Nat Gas occurred.

But let's go back to November 8, when everything still looked up and up. The account had 244 short call options and 26 long calls on Nat Gas. That means the $1,000,000 in equity had to be stretched to cover a net 218 options, which leaves only around $4,600 in equity per short call option. And this doesn't even count the other options on the other commodities with similarly crazy leverage! In any case, we saw that the option with the 5.25 strike went to a $7,000 loss. With only $4,600 per contract in the account, it was lights out on November 14! The options exchange forced the liquidation.

3: Have a risk model but totally ignore it

The co-founder of OptionSellers.com claims to have developed a risk model. He suggested that if you trade short strangles in 10 different commodities, simply assign a risk budget of 5% to each commodity and keep an additional 50% of the principal as a reserve. Seems reasonable: If there's a "rogue wave" in one of the commodities if wipes out no more than 5% of your capital.

In the following chart, you can see how different uncorrelated assets reduce the risk.

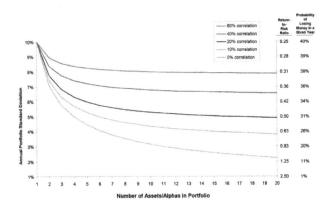

So, were they even sticking to their naïve risk model? Apparently not! The risk budget for Natural Gas would have been only $50k (=5% of $1m), which amounts to just about $230 per short Call option or about a $0.023 move in the option price. That $230 loss was breached on November 9, it had grown to $460 on November 12 and $1,700 on November 13. They already needed to cut their positions as early as November 9, and certainly on November 13. But they didn't! They had suffered some moderate losses by November 12 and significant losses by November 13 and they likely wanted to recover the money, risk model be damned! They abandoned their risk model exactly at the wrong time!

Solution:

Selling options and just praying and crossing our fingers that the price will hopefully never move beyond the strike probably works fine most of the time. But not in November. Obviously, the solution is to have a proper risk model and stick to it. If we had to implement their strategy I'd do so by doing a vertical spread rather than a naked short call. In a vertical spread, you'd still sell a call at, say, $5.25 but you'd also have a long call with a higher strike price, say, $6.25 with the same expiration date to hedge the unlimited loss potential. The maximum loss of that position would have been the difference between the strike prices ($6.25-$5.25=$1.00) minus the net income from the option premiums, just under $10,000 per contract. If you're really serious about that risk model where you have only $50,000 risk budget for natural gas, you'd do the vertical spread with only 5 option pairs. Option Sellers had 218 naked short calls, 43.6 times the exposure. And that's to the much riskier short call option without the tail protection!

4: Misunderstand the peculiar features of the contracts you're trading

Commodity futures can and often do deviate wildly from their long-term fundamentals. One bad storm system in the Midwest can wipe out the crop of some ag commodity and send prices up. One hurricane can halt production for Crude Oil and Natural Gas in the Gulf of Mexico and send the respective futures prices into the stratosphere. True, the price will normalize again in the long-term, but if you sold Call options on one of the impacted commodities and prices deviate drastically from long-run fundamentals between now and the expiration date you're screwed.

Know what you're trading! Educate yourself. Don't fall for the slick presentation of a pushy salesman/financial advisor. Just one look at the NG price chart with crazy swings of $10 or more in a short period (potentially a loss of $100,000 per short call option with a multiplier of 10,000!!!) would tell me that you can't sell naked short calls with only $4,600 in margin per contract!

5: Don't bother understanding what your financial adviser is doing

When clients now complain that they had no idea how risky their investment was. A quick look at your brokerage statement would have revealed the crazy leverage these guys were using.

Why did LTCM, and Niederhoffer , LJM, Optionsellers and many others carry such large positions?

At the end of the day it all comes down to <u>greed</u> . It's because traders want to turn a sound strategy that can produce 10% per annum returns into something that generates 30% per annum. And of course the only way to do this is to leverage the capital.

But as we've seen time and time again, the more you leverage the higher your chances are of ending the game bankrupt.

That's why it's crucial to get position sizing right alongside a solid trading edge and risk management.

The late John Bender explains this perfectly in his interview inside *Stock Market Wizards*.

It might seem that if u have an edge, the way to maximize the edge is to trade as big as you can. But that's not the case, because of risk. As a professional gambler or as a trader, you are constantly walking the line between maximizing edge & minimizing your risk of tapping out.
~ Market Wizard John Bender

We can illustrate this concept with a simple example. Here's a decent "good enough" trading strategy that starts with $10,000 in account equity.

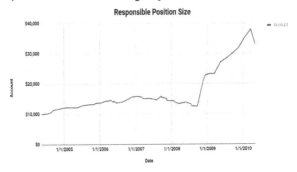

From mid-2004 to mid-2010 it did pretty well. $10,000 turned into around $33,000.

Now here's the exact same trading strategy, with the exact same starting equity, but with 10x the position size.

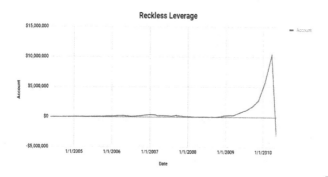

The allure of leverage is obvious. The 10x model at its height had a 1000x gain. $10k turned into $10 million. The prospect of outsized returns is what lures traders to lever.

But it's a farce. Using this amount of leverage guarantees a blow up will occur at some point. And unfortunately for this trader he didn't stop and ended the game with a $3 million debt to the broker.

To position size correctly you need robust risk management assumptions.

That means assuming any product can trade at any price at any time.

If your trading VIX for example, assume it can go from 10 to 100 overnight. That might sound asinine but in reality it keeps you safe. Because at the end of the day anything *can happen*.

By putting extreme scenarios in your universe you can devise a way to survive should it occur. This way of thinking will keep you from botching position size.

Traders that blow up and over lever don't think like this. Instead they use models that rely on past data to estimate "probable" risk.

Throw those methods out. **Historical data means nothing when it comes to risk management**. The future will always bring something more intense than the past. The unexpected can always happen.

Another thing to be cognizant of is that strategies with negative skewness (frequent small wins and large rare losses) are especially tricky to position size correctly.

LTCM, Niederhoffer, LJM, Cordier and that XIV Redditor were all implementing strategies with negative skewness.

If you're strategy has these characteristics it's even more important to run extreme stress testing on your process and assume that your **trading vehicles can trade at any price at any time**[5].

Size your positions from that extreme stress test. Never rely on past historical moves to define your risk in a negative skew trading strategy. **The traders that rely on past data to size up risk always blow up.**

5

Liquid Products

Think deeply about your position sizing process, and remember that if you don't bet, you can't win, but If you lose all your chips, you can't bet[6].

CHAPTER 7: OPTIONS AS RISK REDUCERS

OPTIONS vs ETF/ETN

Options are a powerful financial instrument as they can be used in multi-leg strategies to profit from directional or neutral price biases. Although they may not be as easy to structure as simple buy and hold stock strategies they provide several significant advantages.

The Study:

Compared the most elementary options strategies to a long stock position in the S&P 500.

Short 30 Delta Put (Short Put)
Long 100 Shares + Short 30 Delta Call (Covered Call)
SPY (Long S&P 500)
2007 – 2018

Results:

When we take the time to understand options and a few basic trading strategies we can greatly improve our performance. Applying some basic option trading strategies

---

6   Larry Hite

can reduce our portfolio volatility by up to 30% while only sacrificing a small portion of returns.

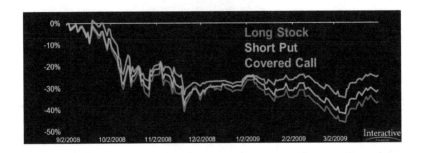

Another Study:

We looked at long putspreads in VXX

From June 2010 to Feb. 2019

Setup: First trading day of the month, 45 Days To Expiration (DTE)

Placed the following trades:

2pt wide ATM put spread

and 5pt wide ATM put spread

The Results:

Long Put Spreads

Held to Expiration	2pt Wide	5pt Wide
P/L	$1,440	$4,476
# of Winners	39 / 50	40 / 50
Average Debit	$1.23	$2.94
Expected Win Rate	61%	59%
Actual Win Rate	78%	80%

Another Study:

VIX call spreads compared to inverse VIX ETFs.

Ultimately the results showed that VIX short call spreads have exhibited more consistent returns than long inverse VIX ETFs.

Credit call spreads in VIX.

The profit potential of these trades is capped at the credit received.

Does it make more sense to utilize an inverse ETF to be short market volatility?

These are two inverse VIX ETFs:

Short VIX Short-Term Futures
SVXY

Daily Inverse VIX Short-Term ETN
XIV

Both of these products seek returns from falling market volatility (decreasing VIX). XIV has no listed options and SVXY options are far lower liquidity than VIX.

2012 - 2018
VIX, XIV, SVXY

Compared

Short VIX Call Spreads (short 50 delta, long 10 delta)

Managed at 50% or held to expiration

Long SVXY stock, Long XIV Stock

Held for same time as the short call spreads

Short Volatility Strategies			
Strategy	Short VIX Call Spreads	Long SVXY	Long XIV
Success Rate	90%	71%	72%
Average P/L	$69	$71	$36
Average Profit	$109	$452	$229
Average Loss	-$309	-$882	-$454
Max Loss	-$742	-$3,924	-$2,006

While all strategies were net profitable, the long inverse ETFs saw huge standard deviations of P/L with a lower success rate.

Now the same study but only enter a position when VIX>
20

Short Volatility Strategies	- VIX Above 20		
Strategy	Short VIX Call Spreads	Long SVXY	Long XIV
Success Rate	98%	86%	86%
Average P/L	$145	$254	$129
Average Profit	$151	$353	$179
Average Loss	-$202	-$331	-$171
Max Loss	-$319	-$1,673	-$865

The long ETFs worked better when isolating high VIX
occurrences, but the success rate still fell short of the VIX
call spreads.

CHAPTER 8:

CONTANGO: THE BEAST OF BURDEN FOR VIX-LEVERAGED BUYERS

They keep pushing and suggesting to traders the buying of volatility as a form of portfolio protection. Be it on Bloomberg or CNBC, the mantra continues in spite of the complacency that has served to underline the Volatility S&P 500 (VIX) over the last couple of months. Unfortunately, when the media outlets discuss buying volatility they do little in the way of detailing how or why volatility should be bought short of saying, "protect your portfolio".

Most individual traders don't realize the reality that ensues after choosing to buy volatility in most form factors, be it directly or through the various VIX-leveraged ETFs and ETNs. It's not just that you, the trader, are buying an instrument that forces timing a volatility event, but it also forces greatly timing an exit of that instrument and before it decays in price once again. This is what the media doesn't explain, at all! Furthermore, just because volatility is forecasted to increase in the near-term by the media, analysts and economists, that doesn't necessarily mean an individual trader can or will benefit from buying VIX and VIX-leveraged instruments.

For example on Dec. 2016 the VIX climbed nearly 4% and if you bought shares of UVXY thinking they would increase in value due to their VIX leverage, you were found wanting for profits as shares declined to new all-time trading lows. If this seems unusual to you because you thought UVXY was a good hedging strategy it's likely because one of its construction variables wasn't considered, contango.

Contango is the defined condition occurring when VIX futures that underlie these ETFs are in price/time arrangement and as such contribute to the share price decay. When the level of contango increases it also exacerbates price declines, even during periods where the VIX actually rises. In more laymen terms, when contango takes over a share price death spiral takes place in the VIX leveraged ETF until the share price exhibits a reset. The reset occurs with an authorized reverse split.

On February 25, 2019 we can see a contango between Mar ch and April contract of 5.36% that means that the ETF will lose at least 5.36% on the contracts that they roll from Mar ch to April 2019

For those looking to hedge against volatility by utilizing VIX-leveraged ETFs, make sure you understand their composition and what level of contango exists before doing so.

For those traders buying UVXY hoping to hedge against the possibility of greater volatility in the future, it would behoove them to understand that UVXY does not own VIX, but rather VIX futures contracts. As such it does not matter that the VIX rises on a particular day. What really matters is the VIX future, a contract that expires on a set date each month. It's not that buying volatility as a hedge can't work in favor of the trader, but rather the timing has a magnified determination in the matter. Moreover, why play the "market timing" game?

Volatility and VIX-leveraged instruments were not introduced to be used from the long side.

The VXXB prospect say:

> *The long term expected value of your ETNs is zero. If you hold your ETNs as a long term investment, it is likely that you will lose all or a substantial portion of your investment.*

http://www.ipathetn.com/US/16/en//instruments.app?
searchType=text&dataType=html&searchTerm=VXXb#/details/341408

The nature of volatility is that of exhibiting longer periods of complacency than it does outsized fear/volatility.

"But what about the financial crisis and what if you had bought the VIX during that time"? This is a question often put forth by those who fear and don't understand shorting the VIX and VIX-leveraged instruments, but it pretty perfectly points toward proving the performance of the VIX.

The vast majority of the equity market declines came in just a few short months whereas the rebound from that period has lasted roughly 9 years or more. A few short months versus 9 years or more. That's how complacent the market is and how it is reflected through the VIX, always. If it weren't exhibited this way, there likely would not be a market to participate with capital. Nobody is putting their money into a state of constant fear and uncertainty, constant being the keyword.

UVXY and like instruments have seen large buying volume outright and through options over the last couple of weeks. As many traders anticipate Dow new highs, these market participants also believe or expect Dow to elicit a market decline from such a level.

It's for this, among other reasons, traders have been buying "protection" against the potential for a return of volatility in the markets near-term. But as I have said for many years, complacency is the greatest value to markets and can persist for longer than most traders can realize or rationalize.

Rationalizing that volatility should have presented itself is easy enough and many traders have convinced themselves that the OPEC decision, Italian Vote, U.S. Elections, S&P

500 trading at 20X, FOMC raising rates all should have elicited greater volatility in the markets and yet all that has occurred has been greater complacency. Dow and S&P 500 PE trading levels still remain standing to benefit from a resurgence of volatility. But for all the VIX buyers over the last 30 days and as UVXY has expressed heightened contango, fighting contango.

Contango virtually guaranteed losses to long positions. The far better option, should one have believed volatility and a downturn in the markets was on the horizon, would have been to short SPDR S&P 500 Trust ETF (SPY). The SPY isn't plagued by a variable such as contango. It's unfortunate that the media doesn't articulate the underlying problems with shorting instruments like UVXY or report on the losses from like hedging strategies, but nonetheless...

Contango is a beast! It's unfortunate that more media outlets don't offer greater commentary on the subject matter and even more unfortunate that amateur market participants are encouraged to publish articles on the VIX and VIX-leveraged instruments. One such article which completely avoids discussing contango while touting a belief that volatility will surge was published an article: "Volatility Will Come Back In A Big Way", suggests that alongside the return in volatility will be a spike in VIX-leveraged instruments like VXXB and TVIX. But these instruments don't track the VIX they own VIX futures contracts and as such don't correlate 1-to-1 as the article would have one assume. VIX –leveraged instruments are not for amateur participation either as authors or traders and beg for greater due diligence.

In closing this chapter, as it pertains to the VIX and instruments like UVXY, TVIX and VXXB , know how they are constructed and how they were designed to behave in the market. Buying instruments requires great timing and

61

as noted in their respective and should not be used for more than day trades. Our annual strategy has always been to increase our short position in the new year and during spikes, then taking profits when shares resume their downtrend. For much of the year I will dedicate greater than 30% of my portfolio capital to UVXY and VXXB short call spreads and Short UVXY and VXXB, and by year's end reduce our exposure thus capturing the greatest of profits from their constant decay.

CHAPTER 9:

Finding a Money Manager

Successful people tend to seek out experts to advise and manage much of their financial affairs, whereas unsuccessful people seem to subscribe more to a "do it yourself" mentality. In an attempt to save money up front by handling legal, accounting, and investing matters on their own, unsuccessful people end up losing money in the long run.

If you were being sued, would you read a book on law and attempt to defend yourself? Would you go through all the ads in the Yellow Pages to find the "cheapest" lawyer you could find? Or would you seek out the best litigation attorney you could find and launch a rigorous defense to dismiss the case and countersue for court costs?

If you needed heart surgery, would you seek out a "discount" doctor—perhaps a first- or second-year intern who agreed to cut you a "really good" deal? Or would you research and interview to find the most experienced, skilled surgeon you could find?

Most people would want to hire the best in either of these situations. Yet, when it comes to money matters, many look to hire the money manager with the "cheapest" commission.

"You get what you pay for" is another piece of timeless wisdom.

This does not suggest that the higher the commission, the

better the money manager. It does suggest that, on the whole, if you want competent advice and guidance, you probably are not going to get it on the cheap. This holds true in almost any profession.

It is true that there always will be a certain portion of traders who possess enough knowledge and skill themselves that they only need an order taker or an online trading platform to place their trades. We also forget that to many, regardless of what they say, making money is not their primary reason for trading. They trade as a hobby or pastime and seek the challenge, excitement, or fun of trading. Going it alone is part of the challenge. There is nothing wrong with this.

WHAT TO LOOK FOR IN A GOOD OPTION SELLING MONEY MANAGER.

Experience

Many Money Managers who start in the business wash out within the first two years. The ones who make it beyond this point must at least have learned how to do something right. To succeed over the long term, a Money Manager has to love what he does and be at least competent in it.

Hopefully, what he loves to do is help his clients trade the markets effectively! Look for a broker who has been around the block. There will always be some young up and comers that may be honest and helpful on the phone, but you don't want them to learn with your account. If you are serious about your trading, especially in the advanced technique of option selling, look for somebody with at least
at least 10 years of experience.

Knowledge of Volatility and Option Selling

You want to hire the best advice you can find. You may have to interview a few before you find one who is friendly to and experienced in volatility and option writing.

Have some good questions, and listen to how he answers them. If she stutters and backtracks or puts you on hold several times to get answers to your questions, you probably have, at best, a neophyte.

Focused on You, Not on Himself

Regardless of whether he realizes it or not, a Money Manager's purpose is to help you to succeed. In talking to him, you should sense that you've found an ally to help you through the course of your option selling investment.

Good brokers know that they're good. In talking to them, you should feel like you're talking to a cool, relaxed professional.

Like any business, the investment industry has good and bad people in it. The good news is that the dishonest or disinterested usually don't last long.

The true professionals in the industry have learned that the only path to long-term success is to put you, the client, first and to build long-term, lasting relationships built on trust.

By an advisor, you are more or less hiring somebody to go to battle for you in the tough, winner-take-all world of options. Especially with the sophisticated vehicle of option selling, you'll need one with competence, honesty, and skill.

But there are some talented people out there who really can make a difference in your trading.

Your job now is to go find one.

We do offer option selling portfolios to individual investors. If you would like more information on working directly with our firm Interactive Financial, you may visit us online at interactivefi.com or contact us at

info@interactivefi.com

Recommended Readings

- Warren Buffett Talks to MBA Students by Warren Buffett

- The General Theory of Employment, Interest, and Money by John Maynard Keynes

- You Can Still Make It In The Market by Nicolas Darvas

- The Richest Man in Babylon - Illustrated by George S. Clason

- Invest like a Billionaire: If you are not watching the best investor in the world, who are you watching?

- Back to School: Question & Answer Session with Business Students by Warren Buffett

- New Trader, Rich Trader: How to Make Money in the Stock Market by Steve Burns

CPSIA information can be obtained
at www.ICGtesting.com
Printed in the USA
LVHW021019060120
642627LV00006B/853